VERSES FROM THE VOID

SHAKTHI THANIGAIVEL

Made with ♥ on the Notion Press Platform
www.notionpress.com

For every heart that dares to love profoundly and embrace itself fully.

Contents

Acknowledgements — *ix*

1. Leaving All I've Ever Known — 1
2. Soul's Infinity — 2
3. I Was A Cursed Ruby — 3
4. A Solitary Moon — 4
5. I Am A Living Paradox — 5
6. Endgame = You — 6
7. The World Became A Bokeh — 7
8. My Little Heartbreaker — 8
9. Lights And Shadows — 9
10. Veil Upon Nature's Face — 10
11. Roman Candle — 11
12. Where Are You The 10 Year Old Me? — 12
13. A Heartfelt Letter To My Best Friend — 13
14. The Love Resonation — 14
15. Life Rushes Like A Stream When You Learn To Swim. — 15
16. A Beacon Of Obsolete — 16
17. Folklore — 17
18. Anam Cara — 18
19. Lilac Threads And Crowded Room — 19
20. Different Paths, Eternal Presence — 20
21. Life's Theme — 21
22. A Forever Season — 22

Contents

23. Song Of Comfort — 23

24. Miles And Mine — 24

25. If It's Meant To Be It Is Meant To Be — 25

26. Living Up To The Kindness — 26

27. If I Were The Sky — 27

28. Muse And Mirror — 28

29. Sunshine Soul — 29

30. Burn To Ashes — 30

31. You Are A Poem — 31

32. The Moon — 32

33. Craziest Revelation — 33

34. Divinity — 34

35. World Is Lucky — 35

36. Greatest Piece Of Art — 36

37. Echoes Of Name — 37

38. Found In Blooms A New Rain — 38

39. Love In Yourself — 39

40. A Mirror's Gaze — 40

41. Deeper And Dreamless Sleep — 41

42. A Sombre Song — 42

43. Ashes Of Myself — 43

44. Sunlight Beams On My Soulless Body. — 44

45. Heaven Of Solitude — 45

46. Solitude: A Sacred Time. — 46

Contents

47. My Dear Journal 47

48. Zero Imperfections 48

49. Protect Your Heart 49

50. Angel Number 50

Acknowledgements

My heartfelt love to all my loved ones who were the sunshine to my darkness. Y'all enabled me to find my journey towards self-love.

1. Leaving all I've ever known

In the path of leaving all I've ever known,
Emotions are raw, a tempest.
Love's a cascade,
care's a flood,
In this new world, where I hang on.
Missing echoes loud, a piercing cry,
In the depths of my heart, an endless void.
Each feeling magnified to the core,
In this realm where I'm a love nomad, forevermore.
This feeling, mine and mine alone,
A whirlwind of emotions in a language unknown to the other
side.

2. Soul's Infinity

In her eyes, I found a serene melody,

Each note was a whisper of love's gentle touch.

With every glance, a symphony would begin,

Sounds of passion in a silent poem.

Lost in the music of her soul's infinity,

I danced to the rhythm of her heart's beat.

3. I was a cursed ruby

You were the gravity that held me closer and pulled me tighter,
even when I was a cursed ruby, forbidden to be touched.
In your embrace, I found solace, an angelic divine,
Your love language, a melody sweeter than any wine.
Each moment with you is a tapestry of life hues.
With each word, your love, I live an eternity of divinity.

4. A Solitary Moon

I'll always feel like an outsider, even among the brightest
constellations,
I stand alone, Like a solitary moon, distant and unknown.
Drawn into orbits, yet apart I remain, A void of insignificance,
amongst the laughters that are shared.
In the midst of all the stars that shine, I cast no glow,
I remain a lone wanderer, lost in the ebb and flow of the energy.

5. I am a living paradox

In shadows of doubt, I seek to embrace,
It is like I am a living paradox.
I wish for happiness like a sunshine soul,
Yet here I am, thinking of things that drown me in tears, an
ocean of overthinking.
Where can I find love, a light so bright,
To sustain me through darkness, to guide me to the end of the
tunnel?
A love everlasting that lends me strength to believe and love
myself.

6. Endgame = You

It's like the whole universe knows, except for you, that we are the endgame,
I could see the love brewing in your eyes every time they look into mine,
In this lifetime, I'll wait and wait for you,
for your words and yourself to immerse in my soul.
When will the atoms of our soul collide?
I smile like a madman every time you talk to me,
My heart finds you irresistible and jumps in joy every time you are around me.
Do you feel the same love?
Embrace my love and my thoughts, my sweetheart,
Let yourself become my world,
let us become two happy, dancing souls in the middle of a vast green valley.

7. The world became a bokeh

You made my fictional world into reality
To my eyes, she was the most beautiful soul I've ever seen,
Every moment her reflection falls on my eyes, It was like the
whole world became a bokeh,
and it was just her and only her in my focus.
She was like a gentle, warm breeze on a cold winter night,
and it was not even any grand gestures,
but those little moments when my eyes always go in search of her
in every room,
the way my favourite song always reminds me of her,
the way she holds my hands and lies down with me on the roof,
watching the stars and the moon.
It's like all the fantasies I had about love came to reality through
her.
She became the purpose of my life that I had sought all my time.

8. My little heartbreaker

Hi there, little heartbreaker,
You call yourself a heartbreaker
when they were the ones that broke down yours.
You say you don't care and love,
never talk about them like they weren't there.
But I see through you,
the little kid in your heart, afraid of the love she gives and never
gets back.
Hold on, though, because one day you'll find that one,
yes, that one!
The one that'll make your heart explode with happiness,
and drown it with all the love you deserve and ignite the true
spirit of yours.
He'll give all that he could and beyond
because he knows there's a radiant sunshine waiting to see the
world beyond that dark, cold shadow.
So, Hi there, my little heartbreaker,
Don't go breaking my heart.

9. Lights and Shadows

My soul roams in the lights and shadows,
seeking goodness in people, making their pain my very own.
But every time I get closer, it is me that ends back with the scar.
And I wonder in the darkness, is it me or them?
Being human confuses me.
Wanting to be alone in my thoughts yet craving for people's
embrace.
In the puzzling flow of life,
it always looks back and tells us the balance between chaos and
peace is where life lives.

10. Veil upon nature's face

You are a veil upon nature's face,
You grace the sun with your silent embrace.
In your mystery, the world finds a gentler pace,
A canvas of quiet, where time can't trace.
You wrap the hills, the trees, and the lakes,
In a softness that the heart resonates.
In your presence, the silence falls,
And in that quiet, nature's true beauty awakes.

11. Roman Candle

A beacon of burden, the very existence of me to everyone.
Chained by expectation they carry on me,
when I hardly who know I am myself.
Fake smiles that bloom like a crescent moon is all you see,
What about the blushes of my scar as tears fall into them?
I'm an invisible memory that awaits and disappears like a
Roman candle ceasing to exist.
The throne of darkness torments me,
As I sit here by myself when all the love I ever got burns like the
passion I have for them.
Yet I still patiently wait,
With shimmering hope where destiny guides my people to the
shore of my existence.

12. Where are you the 10 year old me?

Every day, my hope rots away like a rusting metal.
With grains of fear pounding over my soul,
My heart takes a spin with every breath I take.
Every voice whispers loud, and every word spikes a new wave of
insecurity.
Wrestling the wars of my spirit crumbling down
with every moment I dreamt of keeps vapouring away from me.
Where is the 10-year-old me that hopes with all the innocence
and fights the devil with a smile on his face?

13. A heartfelt letter to my best friend

A heartfelt letter to my best friend,
You might not even know this but you mean absolutely
everything to me,
My love and care transcends to the crazy amounts that numbers
can't even quantify it.
This feeling is unparalleled where I know you gave and continue
to give the best days of my life,
It is a feeling that no celestial energy can possibly ever give me.
You made me realize no matter how many walls or how many
miles is between us,
Even those tidal waves of the ocean can never steal you from me.
We'll always be fine because, at the end of the day, we have each
other's back no matter what.
I don't know if it is luck or destiny but I'm eternally grateful to
be born in time you were too.
You have my whole heart, and you are the drive that pushes me
to be a healthier version of myself.
You are my power, my sunshine and everything I've ever asked
for.

14. The Love resonation

How could we ever be just friends?
When I see you smile wide as your lips form a crescent moon,
My heart pumps twice the amount it is supposed to.
I saw you the other day reading a book,
Immersed in the world of fictitious romance,
I wish you could see that love in me that you feel in them.
Every time I blink when I'm with you,
I beat myself up for all the milliseconds that I miss.
Don't get me wrong, I love our friendship with every inch of my
soul,
But part of me wants more, like the ocean waves needing the
moon.
I never want us to be a passing moment but a forever era.
I know this isn't fair on you and our friendship,
Wish I could help myself not feeling this way,
But my constant struggle of pretending and wanting to be
genuine to you,
How would I ever tell you? How could we ever be just friends?

15. Life rushes like a stream when you learn to swim.

Life rushes like a stream when you learn to swim.
Uncertainties walking up to you when you are learning to live.
Voices are clouding up on you, making you numb when you
want to feel.
Noises are increasing in decibels when you try to find serenity,
As you navigate to find happiness, you end up cherishing the
sadness.
The dream you chase becomes uncertain as you move forwards,
Exhausted from your soul, yearning for the peace you always
wanted.
Listen to me with the hope and the light as I tell you,
"You've got this even through the darkest night."
"You'll figure it all out and trust me you'll be fine. "
Through the gates of hell,
I'll stand by you, no matter what,
Step in, when needed, at any moment as the time ticks closer to
your happiness.

16. A beacon of obsolete

Every mystery became a beacon of obsolete,
your eyes became my treasure of truth.
Deep-dived into your soul,
I was buried with your love and embrace.

17. Folklore

Despair seemed to be glued like a never-ending nightmare,
Tempests and Slaughter became legends of my Folklore.
An unwavering soul always remained,
An amulet of destiny that was ingrained.
Even in the darkest hours the light of her blooms,
An anchor to sail as my life streams.

18. Anam Cara

Our lives weaved, we rolled into each other years ago,
Paths diverged with time's relentless flow.
Yet destiny, it seems, had grand plans,
For you returned with just a simple line.
Bound by shared pain, we found our way,
And now, in years, our bond won't fade.
Time's grasp can't measure what we've found,
A soulful friendship, strong and unbound.
We hold each other with a willing hand,
Through vulnerable times and smiles so rich.
A friendship, soulful, we proudly share,
In your presence, Anam Cara, we find our care.

19. Lilac Threads and Crowded Room

20. Different Paths, Eternal Presence

Our lives, they wander on different trails,
Destiny weaves its intricate details.
Embracing the present, we find beauty's grace,
In every moment, we create our special place.
Wherever I may go, wherever I may be,
Your presence is a constant, as you can see.
In every heartbeat, in the whispers of the breeze,
Your soul resides and puts my heart at ease.
In your presence, my world finds its hue,
No other soul can paint it the way you do.
Life's beauty lies in the bonds we share,
Walking different paths, yet we're here.
You're a gem, a treasure, a gift.

21. Life's Theme

Life's an Art Gallery, an array of Hue,
A vivid blend of souls.
If my life were a mosaic art to share,
You're the piece that completes, so rare.
Without you, I'd be an unfinished song,
A sapphire robbed of its brilliant shine.
An Oil painting void of hue,
A tear without the drop,
Your soul, your love, paints my life's theme.

22. A Forever Season

Seasons change, they say,
Yet, here, it's a constant stay.
In the ever-shifting life,
Our collision formed a timeless sky.
Like a puddle of sunshine, a grace,
In your presence, hope shimmers.
Like the moon's elegance, an unconditional love,
You're that home, encompassing the above.
In your warmth, grace finds a place,
In your love, an eternal embrace.

23. Song of comfort

A warm embrace, like a tight, long hug,
Words of peace, like a gentle tug.
Bullets of care, a shield so strong,
In you is where I find song.
Song of comfort.

24. Miles and Mine

Just like the pleasant beam of the moon,
I can grab your hands that embrace my soul.
Just like the waves of the sea,
I can hear your words getting tattooed in my heart.
Just like the presence of flowers in a garden,
I can feel you right beside me.
From miles and miles away from yours to mine and mine to
yours.

25. If it's meant to be it is meant to be

You showed me if it's meant to be,
The distance doesn't matter,
no disagreements and fights are big enough,
timing doesn't matter,
there will always be space for the love,
the universe finds a way,
to greet and hold,
to hug and be a shoulder,
to talk and laugh,
to walk and be present with each other.
You showed me if it's meant to be,
we'll be there and find home in each other no matter what.

26. Living up to the kindness

Even when I'm a burning walking flame you hold me close,
Even when I'm a frosted tentacle you hug me tight,
Even when I'm a hard rock you put me beside you,
You set standards for friendship so very high I try my all to live
up to the kindness you give me.

27. If I were the sky

28. Muse and Mirror

Halfway past eleven, I realised,
Writing poetries for you wasn't mundane,
You are a muse.
With eyes that mirror the night,
A universe on its own, a captivating stunner.
A wide smile, like a sunshine.
A witty humour, like a symphony for laughter.
A clever mind, like the brilliance of a Van Gough painting.
Place your hand on your chest and feel your heartbeat,
that's the beat of the soul that I love the most in this universe

29. Sunshine Soul

A sunshine soul, radiant and warm,
A beacon of joy in life's ever-changing storm.
Your spirit, a beam that breaks through the clouds,
A burst of energy, where happiness crowds.

30. Burn to Ashes

Trust me on this,
You are quite literally the most important person in my life,
You are Family,
I genuinely believe that my soul resides in yours,
and you have all the space in my soul.
We are in this together, the battles of everyday life,
I'd give it all me to just see you happy and smile,
I'd Burn this world to ashes if needed.

31. You are a Poem

Poems are a beautiful tapestry of Heart, Head and Soul,
As I pen down words, letter by letter, engraving my love on your
soul,
I realized no amount of words in my poetry can be as beautiful
as you are,
You are a poem by yourself, the most beautiful one to ever exist.

32. The Moon

We love the moon like crazy, don't we,
If you had asked me a year ago I'd just have said I just love the
moon,
Right now, she carries so much more than just love,
She is my messenger,
I talk to the moon to carry all my positive energy to you,
When I look at her,
I do know that you'll also be looking at her 12 Hrs 30 minutes
later.
But she does get jealous and happy, you know,
To know she carries my energy to someone who's more beautiful
than her,
But she also loves the way how there's so much love for her from
your beautiful soul.
For Ruth, it was Dandelions,
For me, it is the Moon herself.

33. Craziest Revelation

You know I never had to worry about me time when I was with
you,
My social battery was never zero when It came to you,
It was more like I don't require a social battery to be around you,
Anytime, Anywhere it always is home when you are by my side.

34. Divinity

Sometimes I wondered how peace would feel during death,
Wondered how it would say my last words in front of you,
staring at your moon-like eyes,
Wondered how it would be to feel my last embrace holding your
hands,
Wondered how it would be to feel your warmth for the last time,
hugging you,
Wondered how it would be to whisper my pain away to end,
lying my head on your shoulder,
I'd attain peace knowing I died right there with the presence of a
divinity, my best friend.

35. World is lucky

The world is lucky to have you here,
you're the soul anyone would be lucky to be with.
It is the fact that you don't know how great you are,
The kind blissful souls always don't do they.

36. Greatest piece of art

Sometimes I feel like an imposter calling myself an artist,
As I gaze up and look at you and the love you show me.
The greatest piece of art isn't made on canvas or marble, and it
isn't made from scriptures or books.
It is that gentle heart of yours that carries the carvings of the
most beautiful art ever born, your soul.

37. Echoes of Name

There is something in you calling me,
I miss how that echoes to my ears when you are right next to me.
It was like the words that I'd been longing to hear for centuries,
From the rustic countryside life in the 1600s to the Modern
skyscraper life in the 2000s,
I needed to hear that, feel that deep in my soul.

38. Found in blooms a new rain

In the darker times, a garden found,
Wilted petals on revered ground.
With care and love's embrace, Life returned, slow and grace.
My heart, once full of pain, Found in blooms a new rain.
Self-love grew from roots so deep, In my soul, light shines now.

39. Love in yourself

In shadows, the heart must fight,
To see the good, embrace the light.
In every wound, a strength concealed,
Through self love, the heart is healed.
Embrace yourself, let shadows fly away,
And watch your life in light set free.

40. A mirror's gaze

In mirrors' gaze, don't see the flaws,
But love your soul with gentleness.
Through pain and strife, a heart can heal,
With self-love's warmth, life's joy reveal.

41. Deeper and dreamless sleep

Words piercing through me like arrows,
who's karma is it that haunts me like my own.
Splintered like my fleshes are torn apart by vacancy in my heart.
As I hear all the voices that are clogging my peace,
My feelings are beginning to sleep off.
Yet, in this shadowed abyss, I yearn to escape,
Where echoes of sorrow and regret reshape.
Each breath a reminder of the pain that I keep,
As my soul falls into a deeper, dreamless sleep.

42. A sombre song

From fractured dreams, a sombre song blooms,
every note ridiculed all that is me.
I was trying to find ways,
To brighter dawns and better days.
Every path I took seemed like an illusion,
a mirage of hope that everything will be alright.
Even through a very dark time,
I believed in the light of goodness.
And every step through the illusion became worth the fight
towards freedom,
My dear freedom that let's me dream.

43. Ashes of myself

The deeper I fall in love with the people around me,
I set myself on fire to make them warm at their lowest.
The warmth I've never received all my past,
I spread them as a flaming comfort to them.
As I grew from the ashes of myself,
The inherited trauma that blurred the pathways,
I was finally able to see the line of loving myself,
The love that nurtured through the good people,
It showed me love isn't burning yourself for their wellness.
But the mere presence of yours through every step,
You'd shine like the moonlight and not burn as a flame.

44. Sunlight beams on my soulless body.

In a dark room with no light,
As I lay down passing the night.
Time goes by like ice on daylight,
but my thoughts stay stagnant like webs on an abandoned
fortress.
I wonder when life feels worth living,
where happiness begins,
and why my sadness does not fade?
As I break my wooden wall,
I see cracks through my wall as the sunlight beams on my soulless
body.
In the light of the sunrise,
I found my answer to it all.
The rootedness of happiness and love all in myself,
The journey towards peace begins with self-love.

45. Heaven of Solitude

Everything you'd ever need in your life,
you already have it all in you.
To bask yourself in that glowing presence,
be grateful for everything you have,
and heal yourself in heaven of solitude.

46. Solitude: A sacred time.

The chaos that exists in identifying our time,
we can't see the line between solitude and being alone often.
Solitude, a sacred time.
A choice that lets u find peace and enables growth in the state of
sublime.
Being alone, we yearn for light and warmth from shadows,
But in solitude, well that's where we find the windows,
The window through which we can see the blooming hope.

47. My dear journal

A mood board with all my dreams shining so bright,
All my love exists right here in the purest light.
The thoughts and words, day after day all in you,
As I craft all that is me through you,
My vision becomes clear on what I want to be,
You are my biggest guide to love myself.

48. Zero Imperfections

There is no perfection in any soul or body,
the crackling flaws make you the very soul you are.
Embrace all that you are,
Take in all the changes you see as you grow older,
All the lessons in the light right in front of you,
let yourself be the glowing light for yourself and the people
around you.
To love yourself is to nurture you and your loved ones.
Your worthiness is nobody's to decide but yourself.

49. Protect your heart

Protect your peace, let boundaries show.
Respect your worth, as you continue to grow,
In peace, true strength we find.
Saying no, an art,
Love's light within our eyes.
Protect the heart in your embrace,
Boundaries are all set, with gentle grace.

50. Angel Number

We all fall,

We all suffer.

But nothing's stronger than the action of your mind through
words,

Be the angel number that brings light of an angel in your life
and people around.

Be careful about what you speak; the words you speak are penned
in thoughts.

Give out the love you deserve and let the world find all the love
you want.